Seabeck Reunion

Seabeck Reunion

Seabeck Haiku Getaway
Tenth Anniversary Anthology

Michael Dylan Welch, editor

Haiku Northwest Press

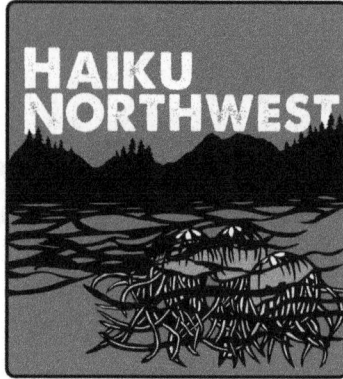

Haiku Northwest Press

Bellevue, Washington

ISBN 978-1-953092-00-7
Copyright © 2020 by Haiku Northwest

This collection of poems commemorates Haiku Northwest's
tenth annual Seabeck Haiku Getaway, October 26–29, 2017,
at the Seabeck Conference Center in Seabeck, Washington.

Thank you to Tanya McDonald and C. R. Manley
for proofreading assistance.
Layout and design by Michael Dylan Welch.
Poems and prose set in 14/20 and 13/18 Constantia.
Headings set in 26/30 Trebuchet MS.

www.haikunorthwest.org

To Johnny Baranski

May 1, 1948 – January 24, 2018

*Longtime friend and attendee
of the Seabeck Haiku Getaway*

passing clouds
the silence of those
no longer with us

Johnny Baranski
Rainsong, 2014 Seabeck anthology

Contents

Welcome 9
    by John Stevenson
Joining the Reunion 13
    by Michael Dylan Welch

Featured Speakers. 21
It Happened at Seabeck 29
Mountain Clouds 47
Autumn Again. 59
In Good Taste 69
Tango 87
Kukai Winners 89

Ten Years of Seabeck Haiku Getaways 97
    by Michael Dylan Welch
Reunion Participants 130

Welcome

Pictures of the Pacific Northwest don't do it justice. They show its beauty but they don't put you in the midst of it—don't give you the scale of it. On my first visit to Seabeck, in 2011, the heights of the landscape instantly thrust me into a childhood frame of mind—towering evergreens surrounding us and the snow-capped Olympics crowding the western horizon. I couldn't help but feel my smallness; how much of my surroundings were "up there" as when I was a child.

Next to this sensation was an old-home feeling, engendered by the warmth of haiku friends and the communal atmosphere of pass-the-dish dining hall meals and shared lodgings. The welcome I received on that first visit was so familial that I have returned many times, feeling somewhat as I once did going home for Thanksgiving when my parents' generation was still living.

By the time of my first visit, the Seabeck Haiku Getaway had undergone several developmental phases. It had outgrown its original venue on the conference grounds and had begun to develop its own traditions and expectations, such as anonymous workshops, lagoon and forest walks, and an entertaining talent show. I am pleased to report that this process of growth and development has continued in more recent years. The retreat recently moved to a fourth, larger space on the conference center campus and all signs indicate that it will need extra room in coming years.

Being a featured guest at Seabeck is an experience I will never forget. The opportunity to compare notes on haiku is always a pleasure but to be at the center of that process once in a while is an unaccountable blessing. I still have the cards from my "haiku sputnik"! All the same, there has been no diminishment in the joy of haiku sharing during my subsequent visits, during which I've been able to sit back more and take it all in.

A key Seabeck tradition has been the announcement of results in the annual Francine Porad Haiku Awards. This celebration has been deeply meaningful to me. Francine was my first friend in the haiku community and an inspiration ever after. I miss her.

It's possible that being an "out of town" participant was especially stimulating in my first couple of retreats. I did already know many of the northwestern American and western Canadian poets but even those I already knew were like new discoveries in the context of Seabeck. To see the simultaneous local and international qualities of the haiku community has been a special reward in my Seabeck experiences.

The selection of guest poets since the retreat began in 2008 has been masterful, in my opinion: a carefully modulated combination of haiku poets of various stripes, scholars, and scholar/poets. A great many people come to be necessary parts of a growing organism such as the

Seabeck Haiku Getaway. As its cofounder and director, Michael Dylan Welch has certainly been a constant. Alice Frampton also cofounded the retreat with Michael. Angela Terry and Tanya McDonald have served as registrars, and many others have made annual contributions of their time and talents. It has been my honor and pleasure to be a small part of this most notable manifestation of haiku community.

John Stevenson
Nassau, New York

Joining the Reunion

"A person with taste is merely one who can recognize the greatest beauty in the simplest things."
—*Barbara Taylor Bradford,* Her Own Rules

When driving to the Seabeck Haiku Getaway each year, often with our retreat's featured guest in the passenger seat, my ritual has usually been to first visit nearby Scenic Beach State Park. We pull into the parking lot, and take at least half an hour, or more if time allows, to walk through the tall pines and yellowing maples down to the small rocky beach. We toss a few stones or oyster shells into Hood Canal, a long reach of Puget Sound, and remark about how high or low the tide is. I note whatever trees in the past year might have tipped into the water from the surrounding embankments, and we admire the view across the sound to the Olympic Mountains, which may have received a dusting of snow by late October. Typically the maples and other trees offer a riot of reds and yellows, with leaves blanketing the trails and the footbridge over the creek. Together we wander to the gazebo, imagine the native rhododendrons in full bloom come spring, and watch for fishing boats out on the water. Sometimes a rainbow welcomes us, and I'm still hoping for a sighting of orcas.

Eventually we amble to the historic Emel house, built in 1912 and remodeled in 1923, where I never fail to ping the giant bell with a fingernail. We talk about the home's history and its connection to Alice Frampton and her family before we stroll back to the car, and I mention how it was Alice who brought us to Seabeck in the first place. Our walking amid the trees and meadows here at the park is a time of decompression, of shifting gears, of melding with the great Pacific Northwest, and of my sharing this beauty and history with our guest for the weekend. We finish this transition by driving from Scenic Beach to the Seabeck Conference Center, rumbling over the old wooden bridge that spans the lagoon between the waterfront and the Historic Inn. And then our haiku weekend begins.

Perhaps this is a ritual for me because our very first Seabeck Haiku Getaway included a visit to Scenic Beach, on October 12, 2008, joined by Alice's mother, Pat Emel. That first year a park ranger led us on a guided tour of the small house with its stunning view of the Olympics. As we explored the porch, the kitchen, the living room, and the upstairs bedrooms, Pat chimed in with personal memories of each room, and Alice told us that her bedroom was the one above the kitchen—she had lived in the house until the age of seven. She later told me that the house's grand stone chimney was built using rocks from the ballasts of lumber ships coming to Seabeck mills nearly a century ago, and that those ships, many from Japan, were responsible for unintentionally importing the now-predominant Pacific or Japanese oyster (*Magallana gigas*). And now here we were bringing haiku from Japan to Seabeck, too. From the

1930s to 1959, the family ran a resort in the acreage around their home, with visitors staying in surrounding cabins. In 1963 the family sold the house and the land to the state of Washington for a new state park, and in 1975 it opened to the public when the park system added campsites and an entry kiosk. Pat's memory is not so good these days (she's about 90 now), and neither is mine, but I am honored to share these narratives, and to continue our fledgling Seabeck haiku traditions in the context of this area's rich personal histories, and the area's even deeper Native American history. And we are pleased, with this anthology, to celebrate the tenth anniversary of Haiku Northwest's annual Seabeck Haiku Getaway.

When I moved to the Seattle area from California in November of 2002, I left behind a tradition of attending the annual Asilomar haiku weekend, run by the Yuki Teikei Haiku Society at the Asilomar conference grounds in Pacific Grove, California. I had participated for twelve years straight, and even timed my move north to attend Asilomar one last time that fall before migrating to Washington. Within a year or so I wished that we might have a similar retreat in the Pacific Northwest. On and off I researched dozens of potential locations and venues, in the mountains or out by the ocean, and in between, but they all seemed too expensive or too far away. Five years went by, and in that time I directed the 2005 Haiku North America conference at Fort Worden in nearby Port Townsend, which kept me from pursuing the retreat idea. The Haiku Northwest group also underwent several changes, especially in 2005 with the passing of its founder, Francine Porad. At the time, Alice Frampton lived in British Columbia, but she moved back to her hometown of Seabeck, Washington in August of 2007 to look after her aging mother. I had first visited Alice in Seabeck in November of 2002, just a week or so after I moved to the Seattle area, when she herself was visiting from Canada, but I don't recall her mentioning the conference center, even though I'd driven right by its old wooden bridge without knowing what it led to. At the time of that first visit I hadn't yet thought about starting a new retreat in the region. I forget when or how I first mentioned it, but several times in the years after that I had told Alice of my ongoing desire to start a new haiku retreat in Washington, and said how I just hadn't found the right place to do it. But this time, in 2007, now that she had moved back home after 34 years in Canada, she said, "Well, how about Seabeck?" That's when she told me about the Seabeck Conference Center, which had been offering reasonably priced retreat and conference facilities to nonprofit groups and organizations since it began in 1915. Alice had even worked in the dining hall occasionally as a teenager. I remember making another trip in July of 2008 to visit Alice and to have a look around the conference center facilities—beautiful heritage and purpose-built buildings scatted around a large and lovely campus with views of the lagoon, the sound, and the mountains beyond. Trails led up into the woods, and deer would regularly meander across lush meadow grass seeking fallen apples in the orchard. I didn't discover it until later, but the Emel name appears on numerous headstones in the historic Seabeck cemetery, a short walk through the woods from the conference center campus. It seemed perfect. We booked two nights for the first Haiku Northwest retreat at Seabeck, which I named the Seabeck Haiku Getaway, and the first retreat took place October 10 to 12, 2008, with Emiko Miyashita visiting from Japan as our first featured guest. Our records show that we had 30 attendees that first year, a number that has mostly risen every autumn since then. What memories we have accumulated in the decade that has passed! You can read more about each of our first ten retreats in this book's afterword, "Ten Years of Seabeck Haiku Getaways."

A principle that has always guided me in planning activities and events at Seabeck is to balance the head and the heart. Haiku is inherently a social poetry, a sharing of emotions and experiences through the images of daily life. Through both reading and writing, these poems naturally appeal to the heart. Yet it is also worthwhile to contemplate technique and craft, which may be said to appeal to the head, or one's intellectual side. In any group of people, it seems advantageous to cater to both emotional and intellectual needs, and to recognize that one focus could benefit people who might neglect the other opportunity. To me, this is part of how one builds and stimulates community. As Wendell Berry once said, "A proper community . . . is a commonwealth: a place, a resource, an economy. It answers the needs, practical as well as social and spiritual, of its members—among them the need to need one another." Indeed, we gather at Seabeck to share and discuss haiku each year because we need each other.

From the beginning, my goal with the Seabeck Haiku Getaway was to make the weekend a hybrid event, partway between a retreat and a conference—with, I hoped, the best of both. Beyond the usual workshops and readings of haiku, over the years various traditions started right away or have emerged and evolved, such as our book fair, silent auctions, anonymous workshops, theme songs, the group photo, haiga exhibits, a kukai (anonymous haiku contest), an anthology, having attendees make their own creative name badges, enjoying walks to the woods and the lagoon, participating in craft activities, and dazzling each other with our talent show. Particular highlights have included the night walk with lanterns (done in silence through a determined rain), and another night walk, to the historic cemetery, on Halloween weekend, where a white-sheathed ghost appeared out of the woods and shared death haiku with us while we stood in a silent semi-circle hearing the sounds of a distant and mournful wooden flute.

Our meeting space changed from Reeser House in our first year to the Lounge A-frame the year after, then for many years at the versatile Colman Center, and most recently at the much larger Meeting House—each move signaling our growth to accommodate an increasing number of attendees and providing more space for our activities. These buildings have shaped our memories. Perhaps the most vivid and sustained highlight from each year, though, has been the camaraderie with friends old and new, whether in our changing meeting spaces or when gathered for shared meals at the round tables that invite group conversation at the Seabeck dining hall. In that spirit, as the leaves turn color each autumn, as the weather begins to turn rainy and melancholy, yet not without celebration, the retreats we hold at Seabeck have become a reunion—a reunion with a beautiful location, a reunion with haiku poetry, and a reunion with cherished friends. We have built a deep camaraderie, and we are delighted to celebrate ten years of Seabeck Haiku Getaway community-building.

The book you now hold in your hands is dedicated to Johnny Baranski. Johnny attended the Seabeck Haiku Getaway with religious fervor, nearly from the beginning, but the 2017 retreat was his last. He died just three months later, after receiving countless messages at his hospice bed from haiku friends worldwide, where his family also surrounded him. In this collection you'll find some of his last published haiku. Those who knew Johnny will fondly remember his broad smile and quiet presence.

Over the years I've felt a pronounced and growing energy at our Seabeck Haiku Getaways. I hope you might also feel it, if you haven't already. I hope, too, that reading this book will feel like joining a welcoming family reunion, or reliving the time we spent together in October of 2017 if you were one of our attendees. We begin with a selection of 20 poems by the ten featured guests from our first decade, and we offer each of them our gratitude for their presence and influence. The poems that follow next appear in four main sections. "It Happened at Seabeck" focuses on specific activities we enjoyed, and includes 40 haiku and senryu. Next comes "Mountain Clouds," a sequence of 21 miscellaneous poems that felt best here rather than in the other three sections. After this comes "Autumn Again," with 19 poems that dwell on the season of waning—the colorful time of year when we've always held our much-loved getaways. And then comes "In Good Taste," with 43 poems celebrating our 2017 weekend theme of taste, one of the senses we've been working through over five years. Here I think of Anthony T. Hincks, who said, "It's when you smell the breeze, taste the salt, and feel the waves beneath your feet that you truly know that you are alive." After this come six poems in a late-night erotic rengay titled "Tango," an outgrowth of Jacquie Pearce's "Erotic Haiku" workshop from 2015, which also produced an erotic rengay at our 2016 retreat. Then, to conclude, we have thirteen poems that placed in our 2017 Seabeck kukai, many of these poems echoing the subjects of earlier sections. That makes for 162 poems if you want to add them up, but you'll find even more in the book's final section that describes each of our ten retreats in detail. At the end, too, you'll find a list of 2017 reunion anthology participants—and we hope that one day you might join our reunion too, if you haven't already. Until then, you can join us by contemplating each of the following poems—smelling the breeze, tasting the salt, and knowing that you are alive.

Michael Dylan Welch
Seabeck Haiku Getaway Cofounder

Featured Speakers

Emiko Miyashita — 2008

Mother's Day
the garden sundial
just past three

rinsing Chinese cabbage
on the back of my hands
new blotches

Penny Harter — 2009

migrating butterflies
cover the names—
war memorial

mother's pastry brush—
stiff bristles bending
more each year

Charles Trumbull — 2010

the bell rings
again the playground fills
with pigeons

October chill
a squirrel browses for food
along the third rail

John Stevenson — 2011

writers conference
from a toilet stall I hear
someone quoting me

a deep gorge . . .
some of the silence
is me

Paul Miller — 2012

widening ring
from a cormorant's dive
too brief this visit

growth rings
on a truckful of pine logs
the day's last light

Marco Fraticelli — 2013

saying goodbye
our shadows
almost touch

vigil for the victims
my daughter's swing
fills with snow

Alan Pizzarelli — 2014

snow piles up
the barber shop pole
spins into itself

in the stream
    a shopping cart
        fills with leaves

Randy M. Brooks — 2015

October light
    I open my ribs
to pray

creek water warm . . .
I swing the grapevine
up to my cousin

Sonja Arntzen — 2016

hiss of surf
our footprints no sooner made
than gone

dark cedars
quiet with snow . . .
the mountain's weight

Scott Mason — 2017

one way
into the labyrinth
a maple key

how deer
materialize
twilight

It Happened at Seabeck

Seabeck reunion
crows gather
on the horseshoe pitch

Jacquie Pearce

deer tracks
at the lagoon's rim
rustle of heron wings

Susan M. Kerr

sailboats bobbing
in the Seabeck marina—
new moon

Michael Dylan Welch

white fog fingers
lift up forest ridgetops
old Seabeck highway

Dorothy Avery Matthews

low lagoon tide
under the muddy slick
inch-long fish

Richard Tice

writing poems
on the floating dock
gull tracks

Dianne Garcia

those rosehips
just beyond your reach . . .
falling in the lagoon

Julie Emerson

Seabeck ginko—
picking up shells
on the sandy shore

Ida Freilinger

Seabeck
words
fill the lagoon

Lynne Jambor

after sumi-e
the glide of a mud shark
in the lagoon

Jacquie Pearce

Seabeck Pizza—
on the water's edge ravens
sort through debris

Barbara Ellen Hay

Bolero
beneath it all
the drum

Kay L. Tracy

the dinner bell
in case you didn't hear
the dinner bell

Jessica Tremblay

around the table
wide-ranging conversation
about mashed potatoes

Lynne Jambor

tortilla soup
without avocado
rich conversation

Jim Rodriguez

stillness of woods
broken by leaf fall
sister chatting in my ear

Susan M. Kerr

layered conversation . . .
I take another bite
of mashed potato

Jacob Salzer

morning meditation—
lagoon reflections
waver with the wind

elehna de sousa

meditation . . .
the small chapel door opens
to the mountains

Lynne Jambor

guided meditation
spontaneously
a tree looks in

Kath Abela Wilson

morning meditation—
in the darkness I find
my center

Barbara Ellen Hay

I contemplate
image within image
the mandala rotates

Connie Hutchison

etegami:
coloring my pumpkin
outside the lines

Barbara Snow

the old sumi brush
regains its point quickly
in his mouth

Julie Emerson

etegami
the gift
of imperfection

Jessica Tremblay

cathedral in the woods
overcast sky
wet seats

Rick Wilson

on the bouncy bridge
an unknown force
rocks it

Ida Freilinger

anonymous haiku—
a gin-less brew of tonic
and bitters

Nancy Bright

seeing
the whiteboard
through her glasses

Jim Rodriguez

kitemaking workshop
I blame my failure
on lack of lipstick

Kath Abela Wilson

the instructor's haiku kite
flies better than mine . . .
windfall apples

Michael Dylan Welch

my indoor kite
twirling through a sky
with no wind

elehna de sousa

the kite builder
makes
the wind

Jessica Tremblay

after his ode to Cheetos
this urge
to lick my fingers

Tanya McDonald

autumn rain
the rhythm of his fingers
on the tabla drum

Michelle Schaefer

improv—
playing
by the seat of my pants

Terry Ann Carter

family plot
granite slabs sloping away
from each other

Connie Hutchison

old cemetery
headstones wreathed
in perpetual growth

Scott Mason

squirrel midden
a blanket of seed bracts
at the infant's gravestone

Connie Hutchison

Bolero playing
on and on in my head
crescendo of fall leaves

David Berger

Mountain Clouds

fog's advance—
the shape of the glass
in my hand

Dianne Garcia

two wine glasses
leaning on each other . . .
morning fog

Eileen Coughlin

woodsmoke lingers
at the state park campground
closed for the season

Dorothy Avery Matthews

in duckweed
          a channel
full of stars

John Stevenson

glinting rivulets
braiding down the mountain
remembered thoughts

David Berger

ferry dock rain or shine Jehovah's Witnesses

Terran Campbell

road trip
dad let me
hold the map

John Stevenson

secret ingredient
in the family stew
adopted newborn

Kath Abela Wilson

from out of the earth
an old child's truck
missing wheels

Shelley Baker-Gard

dahlias
and promises
rusting

Lysa Collins

jacks toss
how we remember
childhood

Terry Ann Carter

the memory of your hand
eats a hole
in my heart

David Berger

fishing pole
the only bite
odonata

Ellen Ankenbrock

fiddleheads
slowly unfurling
a rhapsody in C

Angela Terry

standing ovation
the steady beat
of cricket song

Kay L. Tracy

a doe and two fawns
perhaps I'll turn
vegan

Johnny Baranski

tarantula—
barefoot in the bathroom
I make up a new dance

Barbara Ellen Hay

at night they come
zombie squirrels
for my strawberries

Richard Tice

lifting its leg
on the news of the day
my dog comments

Marion Davidson

wavelets . . . .
the mathematics
of shadow and bright

Dianne Garcia

an infinity of prime numbers . . .
pine trees fading
into mountain clouds

Angela Terry

Autumn Again

wind-blown leaves—
realizing I now
use handrails

Gary Evans

a steady stream
of golden leaves . . .
poetry in motion

elehna de sousa

autumn leaves
randomly descend—in space, time
to destined spots

Susan M. Callan

early autumn even in sadness morning star

Terran Campbell

a lone goose honk
giving voice to the dark
no moon

Michelle Schaefer

autumnal light
shadows and thoughts
stretch

Gary Evans

rushing to see
the song out my window
fall migrations

Shelley Baker-Gard

my children see
the face within—
uncarved pumpkin

Michael Dylan Welch

the rust line
        on our toilet tank—
autumn deepens

Scott Mason

heavy autumn rain
the revived creek bed
conducting a chorus

Dorothy Avery Matthews

the fall night air
resounds with the owl's call . . .
but to whom to whom

Susan M. Callan

sleepless autumn night
footsteps in the hall—
diagnosis cancer

Rayn Roberts

fall peak it's all downwind from here

Scott Mason

here and there
painting the fog gold
broadleaf maples

Richard Tice

dressing for fall
a necklace of sapsucker holes
around the poplar

Jacquie Pearce

stripping
from top to bottom . . .
autumn maple

Susan Constable

pebble lodged
in a gnarled tree root
growing old together

Susan M. Kerr

applefall—
the glistening black
of deer scat

Vicki McCullough

the thud
as two apples hit the ground—
I leave one for the deer

Vicki McCullough

In Good Taste

barrel-aged stout—
all these years
we've been together

Tanya McDonald

fermented apples
a taste of cider
in the air

Johnny Baranski

coffee high . . .
the snail pace
of clouds

Nicholas Klacsanzky

renowned editor
reveals the only source
beach shack lattes

Nancy Bright

steaming coffee
a poet pens
in silence

Ruth Marcus

tea poured
friends linger
at the table
I built

Ellen Ankenbrock

slowly waking . . .
honey and cinnamon tea
this chilly morning

Kathleen Tice

almond moon
above the rooftop café
steaming chai

Ruth La Sure

jasmine
in my tea
butterflies waken

Kay L. Tracy

dry twigs crackle
in the fireplace—
rainflower tea

Lysa Collins

my cup of tea
the taste
of a falling leaf

Janet Whitney

crushed ice and a lemon wedge—
I sip
into summer

Lysa Collins

tea and gingersnaps . . .
the afternoon she forgot
my name

Angela Terry

nettle tea—
gradually we all arrive
in the same place

Nicholas Klacsanzky

nettle cheese soup the sting of winter

Eileen Coughlin

nettle soup
after the sting
I am avenged

Laura Quindt

fallen leaves
the crunch in my
breakfast cereal

Johnny Baranski

sunrise . . .
the glass fills
with orange juice

Jacob Salzer

dewy web
morning paths converge
for cinnamon rolls

Barbara Snow

cream of wheat—
the confessions
I keep

Nicholas Klacsanzky

early frost
warm gingerbread under a blanket
of autumn applesauce

Laura Quindt

hot and sour soup
the woodsy flavor
of autumn mushrooms

Kathleen Tice

autumn sun
orange peel spray
glistens

Gary Evans

sweetness of blackberries—
the wounds still
run deep

Kathleen Tice

winter holidays
pine trees chestnuts relatives
fruitcakes

Rayn Roberts

the cutting knife
slices through chocolate icing
reflection

Darlene Dihel

knifing the chocolate cake—
you take two helpings
despite the diagnosis

David Berger

new friends chatting
the menu includes
sweet and sour

Ruth Marcus

drizzle on the sound
looking forward
to the cold salad bar

Rick Wilson

his explanation
longer than my bowl
of potato-leek soup

Barbara Snow

heedless of the chitchat
bubbles of white foam
fill the to-go cup

Marion Davidson

the taste of razor clams
dark memories
of my childhood

Janet Whitney

home sick—
the sandy sweetness
of cinnamon toast

Tanya McDonald

these mildewed leaves . . .
the huckleberry tang
of my youth

Vicki McCullough

coughing
we know
who tasted
the hot sauce

Connie Hutchison

my father
joins the conversation
red pepper relish

Susan Constable

soaking rice
I still do things
dad's way

Michelle Schaefer

a recipe
in my mother's hand
comfort food

Susan Constable

supplements
grandson feeds me
the red one

Shelley Baker-Gard

blotting muffin crumbs
on my napkin
none left for the fly

Laura Quindt

ripe peach
mouth full of sweetness
summer day

Ruth La Sure

sugar
on the last cookie . . .
snowstorm

Jacob Salzer

in the air
the taste of salt
home again

Janet Whitney

Tango

midnight—
you roll over
and wake to the moon   *David Berger*

    my kisses follow
    the curve of light   *Jacquie Pearce*

our legs entwined
wordless
we fall to the floor   *Michael Dylan Welch*

    a tease of breasts
    and squeeze below   *Michelle Schaefer*

my tongue
in your mouth
you draw me in   *James Rodriguez*

    rising on the sultry air
    the yowl of a cat   *Vicki McCullough*

Kukai Winners

First Place

deviled eggs
seasoned with paprika
and mom's opinions

Dianne Garcia

Second Place

abandoned dock
a crow checks
the crab trap

Jacquie Pearce

Third Place (tie)

red laser light
the mathematician's thoughts
dancing

      Vicki McCullough

sturgeon moon
bigger and bigger
the one that got away

      Johnny Baranski

Fourth Place (tie)

laughter
in the group photo
lagoon ripples . . .

Jacob Salzer

Seabeck washroom—
admiring her shoes
beneath the stall

Terry Ann Carter

Fifth Place

cumulus
whatever
moves you

Scott Mason

Sixth Place (tie)

morning coffee
the fog slowly lifts
on the lagoon

Barbara Ellen Hay

windfall apples—
the taste of fog
on my tongue

Michael Dylan Welch

road hum
our elbows touch
and touch

Barbara Ellen Hay

Seventh Place (tie)

pinwheel—
no wind
on the grave

Susan Constable

stars above you unfold into my arms

David Berger

tide pool
wherever we aren't
clams spitting out water

Richard Tice

Ten Years of
Seabeck Haiku Getaways

by Michael Dylan Welch

Haiku Northwest's annual Seabeck Haiku Getaway celebrated its tenth annual retreat in October of 2017. What began as a shorter weekend tradition in 2008 quickly stretched into a long weekend, and over the years we've added new and varied traditions. Perhaps the talent show was our most dramatic addition, but even smaller traditions, such as weathergrams or the "haiku sputnik," have contributed to the weekend's flavor. What follows, to commemorate our tenth anniversary, is an overview of each of Haiku Northwest's first ten haiku retreats at the Seabeck Conference Center in Seabeck, Washington. While not every activity is listed, these reports cover a great majority of each weekend's numerous highlights, with gratitude to everyone who helped to make them happen.

2008

For the first retreat in 2008, our theme song was Sarah McLachlan's "Ordinary Miracles" ("everything is beautiful— / it's just another ordinary miracle today"), a fitting lyric for how haiku celebrates the ordinary miracles of everyday existence. As our featured guest, Emiko Miyashita from Japan led an introduction to haiku from a Japanese perspective, and surprised us by wearing different kimonos during the weekend. With Michael Dylan Welch, she read poems from the recently published Gendai Haiku Kyokai Anthology, *The Haiku Universe for the 21st Century*. She also talked about "Santōka's Traditional and Free-Verse Haiku," sharing selections of her translations done with Paul Watsky. Other highlights were a "Haiku Show and Tell" group activity led by Ruth Yarrow, a "Details of Japan" slide show and "Fuyoh Observations: Six Lessons from Japanese Haiku" presentation by Michael, plus Christopher Herold's two-part workshop, "Feathering the Moment: Spontaneous Composition Emanating from Silent Observation." Christopher later collected poems from this collaborative exercise in a small booklet that might be considered our first unofficial retreat anthology, or at least a precursor to this tradition. Margaret Chula led a haibun workshop, and Alice Frampton talked about "The Music of Haiku" and facilitated an outdoor scavenger hunt. We also began our tradition of having anonymous haiku workshops, where poems without names are written on a whiteboard for group discussion. This first year we also had a friendly competition for best name badges. Over the years we've each made our own, with great creativity and variety (plus, ahem, a sticky note or two). We no longer continued the competition after this first year, but do continue to revel in the creative ways attendees have identified themselves. In later years we've had as many as 10 to 20 newcomers each year, so name badges have been very helpful. In our first year nearly all attendees came from Washington State, but in later years we welcomed participants more and more from Canada, from Oregon and California, and from farther east on the continent—and once or twice from Australia.

We held our 2008 meetings in Reeser House, our chairs arranged in a large circle that taxed the room's limits. On the Sunday afternoon we all visited Scenic Beach State Park to explore the woods, the waterfront, and the old Emel house where Seabeck Haiku Getaway cofounder Alice Frampton lived as a child. Michael and Alice codirected this first retreat, and the registration fee was $139, including accommodations (Friday and Saturday nights), and all meals and activities. This first year we made $203 on the silent auction, which was just enough for us to break even on our expenses, and these silent auctions have been a great benefit ever since. Here's a poem by Emiko from the first Seabeck Haiku Getaway weekend:

> Reeser House's bathtub
> still warm, I wonder who took the bath
> before me

2009

Our second retreat took place October 16–18, 2009, in the Lounge, an A-frame building with large triangles of windows at each end. Partway through the weekend we marveled at how, for at least ten minutes, it was raining at one end of the short building but not at the other! Tanya McDonald joined Michael in directing this retreat, and they continued to run the next few retreats together, with Tanya serving as registrar, taking on the challenge of making sure everyone got into the accommodations they needed and had their dietary restrictions met. The weekend's theme song was "Bread and Roses" by Judy Collins ("Hearts starve as well as bodies; give us bread, but give us roses"). The registration fee was $159, and we had 33 attendees. Penny Harter was our featured guest, and with Penny we began a new tradition of starting the weekend with a reading by our guest, this time titled "Haiku Hopscotch: From Haiku, to Sequences, to Haibun." Down at the beach, Penny also skipped her first stone ever. She also led a haibun workshop and facilitated a Hubble telescope photo workshop, with dozens of space photos scattered on the floor for us to pick up and write about—or be inspired to write about whatever came to mind. Another new tradition was our first annual Seabeck kukai, or haiku contest. We each wrote haiku anonymously on index cards and then we chose and discussed our favorites—it was a pleasure to find out who wrote the winning poems. Other highlights included a discussion led by Ce Rosenow on "The Haiku Society of America in 2010 and Beyond" (Ce was president of the society that year), an exploration of Southern California season words by Deborah P Kolodji, with the suggestion that we might nurture a similar awareness with Pacific Northwest seasonal references. In addition, Richard Tice gave a presentation on "What Might Have Happened When Sōchō and Bashō Wrote Linked Verse?" Margaret D. McGee also gave a talk from her recent book, *Haiku—the Sacred Art*. We also wrote tan-renga together, later collected in a booklet, and Michael gave a presentation on "Learning from Shugyō Takaha." Tanya led another "Haiku Show and

Tell," during which time Genie Nakano danced some haiku for us, among many other fascinating revelations. Dejah Léger also recorded a magical video of each of us reading our haiku, which we were happy to share on social media and on YouTube after the weekend.

Another standout from the weekend was the production of our first official retreat anthology. In fact, we made two. Tanya McDonald edited *Woolly Bears and Cedar Flashing*, collecting haiku, senryu, and haibun written during the weekend. Michael edited *Seeing Stars*, assembling "galactiku" poems written during Penny's Hubble telescope workshop. Both books were hand-sewn, and *Seeing Stars* later won the "Best Anthology" award in 2010 in the Haiku Society of America's Kanterman Book Awards, for all haiku books published in 2009. Old-time Seabeck attendees still rave about Penny's remarkable and inspiring workshop. The following is one of Penny's poems:

> so many stars—
> how can we be lonely
> in their light

2010

In 2010, Charles Trumbull was our guest speaker, over the weekend of November 4 to 7. For the first time we started on Thursday afternoon. The extra night bumped our registration fee up to $199, and we've kept the retreat to three nights since then. We also moved to the Colman Center for the first time, to accommodate our 39 attendees. We met upstairs in a large circle of chairs, and used the downstairs room for other activities. "Seize the Day" by Carolyn Arends was our theme song ("Seize the day, seize whatever you can / 'Cause life slips away just like hourglass sand"), reminding us to make the most of life's moments that make up the warp and weft of haiku. Charlie gave detailed presentations on "Meaning in Haiku" and "The Uses of Haiku: Native American Writers." Other presentations were "Haiku with Very Few Verbs" by Jerry Ball, "Exploring Urban Haiku" by Deborah P Kolodji, "The Seasons in Kigoless Haiku" by Christopher Herold, and "Punctuation in Haiku," a workshop by Michael. Tanya McDonald walked us through her workshop, "Juxtaposition: Taking a Flying Leap," and led us on "Favorite Haiku" and "Haiku Show and Tell" group sharings. Susan Constable's haiga slideshow, "In and Out of Water," brought the art of haiga to our increased attention, and we've continued to have haiga displays and presentations in most subsequent years. Ce Rosenow directed a workshop on prose poetry and haibun and gave a presentation on "(Re)Defining the West: Orientalism in American Haiku." Christopher and Michael also led renku writing sessions.

A particular highlight from the weekend was a craft activity led by Susan Callan in making suminagashi, or ink marbling on fancy papers. The 2010 handmade retreat anthology, *From Leaf to Leaf*, edited by Tanya and Michael and with illustrations by Dorothy Matthews, featured suminagashi paper on each unique cover. This year was also the first year we hung what we call the "haiku sputnik" in our meeting room—a sphere with dozens of haiku on index cards clipped to the ends of metal antennas. From the start it was always a pleasure to see our featured guest discover that all of the sputnik's poems were his or hers. Outside the Colman Center meeting location we also enjoyed the brand new "Bouncy Bridge," a short suspension bridge stretched across a shallow gully, which led to many moments of laughter, and poems as well. For the first time this year, we also presented the results of the Porad Award haiku contest, sponsored by the Washington Poets Association but recently taken over by Haiku Northwest. Here's one of Charlie Trumbull's haiku from the weekend, with its Bashō allusion:

> writing exercise
> in the distance
> a duck calls, whitely

2011

For 2011, still at the Colman Center, we met over the weekend of October 13 to 16, with John Stevenson as our guest. He had taken the train all the way from upstate New York to join us. As usual, the fall colors were out in full force. We had 31 attendees, and our registration fee was again $199. Our theme song, "Bound by the Beauty," came from Jane Siberry ("I'm bound by the beauty of light upon the land / Oh, I'm bound by the beauty of the wind"), echoing the delight that surely all haiku poets feel in response to the world around them. John led us in three workshops that helped us recognize the world's beauty, and its darkness, including improvisational writing. Michael Dylan Welch led "renkurama" and rengay writing sessions, and gave a talk on "21 Haiku Lessons from *A Book of Tea*." Carmi Soifer led us on a haiku walk focusing on our five senses, and Susan Constable gave another presentation and slideshow on "Photo Haiga: Getting Started."

Barbara Snow also introduced us to weathergrams, which we've been making ever since—haiku in calligraphy, done on strips of biodegradable paper, hung with string on bushes and trees around the campus. And it's from Barbara's presentation, I believe, that this tradition has spread to the larger haiku community, with weathergrams making common appearances at many other haiku events across the continent. As far as I can tell, this happened only after their introduction at Seabeck. The Seabeck staff has told us how they and other guests have enjoyed finding these poems here and there around the grounds for months afterwards.

Meanwhile, as usual, we also held our book fair and silent auction, the latter of which has continued to help raise money for our expenses—our gratitude to everyone who has donated whatever they can, this year and in all subsequent years. And for our anthology this year, we went with a holographic option. This meant that each poet hand-wrote one of his or her poems on special paper designed for custom boxes. The poems were assembled into individual boxes, titled *Bound by the Beauty*, and given to each attendee. Here is a Seabeck poem by John Stevenson:

> bouncing foot bridge—
> I let go of
> my dignity

2012

October 11 to 14 in 2012 saw us returning for our fifth anniversary retreat. Our attendance jumped to 51 people, our highest yet, despite an increased registration fee of $215. Our theme song was an instrumental for the first time— "Gathering" by Chris Spheeris, celebrating the joy of our being together. This time Paul Miller was our featured guest. He led us in a fun and informative workshop, "Haiku Mad Libs." He also gave presentations on "Synesthesia in Haiku," or sense-switching, and on "The Space Between," about the different ways we can create space in the juxtaposition of two parts in our haiku.

We also started a new tradition by having a panel discussion, this first time exploring "Poetic Truth," with Cara Holman, Tanya McDonald, Angela Terry, and Michael Dylan Welch sharing their thoughts on authenticity in haiku. One panel discussion wasn't enough, though. We also explored "The What and Why of Gendai Haiku," with Johnny Baranski, Barry George, Tanya, Paul, and Michael as panelists. I'm not sure we got to the bottom of many questions regarding gendai (modern) haiku, some of which is surreal, opaque, and avant-garde, but we certainly tried.

Other presentations were "Online Haiku Resources" by Cara, "Everything You Always Wanted to Know About Syllables" by Michael (about why counting 5-7-5 syllables is not exactly logical for haiku in English), and digital haiga projections by Terri L. French, Carole MacRury, Annette Makino, Jim Swift, and Michael. For beginners this year, Michael offered his "Introduction to Haiku" workshop, while Tanya led one of our anonymous workshops—and

Johnny Baranski led another anonymous workshop later. Tanya also facilitated a bookmaking workshop with hand-folded papers. We had another scavenger hunt to get us outdoors, and then shared our discoveries—and sometimes poems. Ruth Yarrow also led us on a stimulating nature ramble—the "Woods and Water Ginko" (haiku walk).

A focal point for the weekend was a sumi-e and haiga demonstration by Fumiko Kimura, where we all tried our hands at brush painting. This art exercise was in association with another new tradition, a display of haiga by members of the Haiga Adventure Study Group of Puget Sound Sumi Artists. We enjoyed their wonderful artwork set up on easels not only in the Colman Center but also in the dining room, where other conference center visitors could enjoy them. We have been fortunate to have the same group provide marvelous haiga exhibits for us every year since, coordinated by Dorothy Matthews and others.

We also enjoyed haiku readings by Barry George, Terri L. French, Alison Hedlund, Margaret D. McGee, Carmi Soifer, Doris H. Thurston, and Annika Wallendahl, beginning a new tradition of having featured readings by selected attendees. Speaking of Doris, another fond memory of this weekend was hearing her play piano during a break when she thought no one was listening.

As usual, we announced the Porad contest winners (this time with flute music by James Rodriguez, who has done this repeatedly since this year) and held another kukai. Cupcakes with autumn-orange frosting helped us celebrate our fifth annual retreat, to go along with a PowerPoint presentation with photos and retreat highlights put together by Michael. Somewhere during the weekend we also had a hokey-pokey break, all putting our best foot in and shaking it all about.

Our biggest new retreat addition, though, was the Seabeck Talent Show. Our MC was Dejah Léger, and if any of us remembers anything from the evening's tremendous variety and fun, it would have to include the worldwide premiere performance of "Ku Contemplator" by Terri L. French, to the tune of Sade's "Smooth Operator," complete with air saxophone by Raymond French. We also witnessed dancing, storytelling, guitar duets (Dejah and Stuart Zobel), dramatic monologues, Broadway musical showstoppers, flute, piano, poems longer than haiku, some bad and not-so-bad jokes, and . . . a crankie. If you don't know what a crankie is, it's a storytelling art-form where a long scroll of paper is "cranked" from one spool to another in front of a bright light, showing silhouetted illustrations, usually while a story is told, sometimes with music. Singing in French, Dejah presented a very detailed crankie that she had been working on for months, a foretaste of another special crankie that we would enjoy the next year.

Our retreat anthology for 2012 was *Windfall*, edited by Connie Hutchison and Ruth Yarrow, but really a team project. Dianne Garcia did layout, and Connie Hutchison provided book design. The collection also included sumi-e by Fumiko Kimura and Frank Kawasaki, and photography by Nick Felkey and Michael Dylan Welch. Each book was hand-bound with bamboo and waxed linen into handmade mulberry paper covers, with fold-out pages for art and the group photo, a truly stunning keepsake of the weekend.

As with each of these weekend descriptions, I'm not able to mention everything, but you can see that our first five years showed the Seabeck Haiku Getaway to be expanding and maturing in exciting ways. Here is a poem by Paul Miller from our fifth annual Seabeck haiku weekend:

visitor myself
a freighter ballasted
with distant sea water

2013

We began our next five years of annual Seabeck haiku retreats over the weekend of October 10 to 13, 2013, still at the Colman Center. We gathered 49 attendees, and the registration fee remained at $215. Our theme song was Louis Armstrong's "Wonderful World." In previous years we played recordings of theme songs, but this year we heard the song live on piano, played by our featured guest, Marco Fraticelli. He also sang the lyrics, which many haiku poets surely love ("I see skies of blue and clouds of white, / the bright blessed day, the dark sacred night, / and I think to myself, what a wonderful world"). Marco was particularly excited to be featured at Seabeck, and his warmth and enthusiasm were infectious. In addition to the customary opening-night poetry reading, he also gave a presentation on "The Haiku Moment vs. the Hallmark Moment" and summarized his King's Road Press books, including a gift for everyone of *Square in the Circle*, a new anthology that offered selected poems by each of the poets featured in his long-running series of publications by leading haiku and senryu poets writing in English.

Marco's main presentation, though, was a screening of *Celesta Found*, a 2003 documentary movie by his sister, Rina Fraticelli, about his accidental discovery around 1972 of a cardboard box in an abandoned log cabin in the Eastern Townships of Québec. The box contained paper, scraps, grocery lists, funeral notices, tax receipts, and seven diaries—all dating from the years 1895 to 1916. This screening was followed by Marco's book launch of *Drifting*, an innovative collection of haibun using actual diary entries by Celesta, appended with his new haiku, entering into the voice of the diary's characters. He was helped in this dramatic performance by Terry Ann Carter, in costume as Celesta, reading diary selections. Marco followed this dramatic performance with a workshop on writing haibun.

As an icebreaker this year we had the "Haiku Bingo" activity, and again enjoyed renkurama collaborative writing. We gained inspiration from anonymous workshops led by Richard Tice, Tanya McDonald, and Michael Dylan Welch. Other presentations included "The French Revolution" by Jessica Tremblay (an overview of French-language haiku activity), a "How Long Is a Moment" workshop led by Michael (he also provided another beginner workshop), an "Invitation to Tanka Reading and Writing" session by Kozue Uzawa, and a haiku writing workshop, "Emily Carr's Wild Flowers," given by Terry Ann Carter. Still more presentations from the weekend included "Telling Family Stories" (haibun) by Dianne Garcia, "Time Travel with Haiku," a writing workshop led by Jacquie Pearce, and "Becoming the Leaf: A Haiku by E. E. Cummings" by Michael. As our first cartoonist-in-residence, Jessica Tremblay also talked about her haiku comic, "Old Pond Comics," and shared several new comic strips about our haiku weekend (she worked late into Saturday night to finish these for us on Sunday morning). We also had a memorial for Jay Gelzer, a beloved member of Haiku Northwest. She loved coming to Seabeck, and had died shortly after our 2012 retreat.

One of the weekend's most memorable highlights was "Entering the Labyrinth: Making and Walking a Spiral Labyrinth," a presentation by Margaret D. McGee. After Margaret talked about the history and varieties of labyrinths, she led us outside to construct one ourselves, on the lawn beside the Colman Center. We gathered branches and leaves and other natural materials from the woods, worked together to lay out a labyrinth, and decorated it with our haiku (on weathergrams). We then walked the spirals meditatively—naturally falling into silence as we walked. This exercise prompted the writing of many haiku, which found their own special section in the 2013 retreat anthology, *A Warm Welcome*, edited by Michael Dylan Welch and Angela Terry, with artwork by Annette Makino. We've often used one of Annette's paintings of the Seabeck sign to publicize subsequent Seabeck retreats, and have used the same painting on Facebook as the Seabeck Haiku Getaway profile image.

We also heard haiku readings by Susan Constable, Vicki McCullough, Annette Makino, Carmen Sterba, Terry Ann Carter, and Johnny Baranski, the latter with piano accompaniment from Marco. We also revealed the winners of the 2013 Porad haiku contest, celebrated the winners of another annual Seabeck kukai, and had Alice Frampton lead us on a walk through the woods, rife with wild mushrooms and falling maple leaves, to the historic cemetery at the edge of the Seabeck conference grounds. This walk also inspired poems that found their own section in the 2013 retreat anthology.

And we enjoyed another spectacular talent show on Saturday night, again MC'd by Dejah Léger. Following up on her much-loved crankie performance in 2012, this year she had all attendees contribute to making a new crankie, writing their haiku on a long scroll, which we celebrated with much delight, reading the poems aloud as they scrolled past the light. Another highlight was the ukulele chorus, but how could we forget the belly dancing, magic tricks, storytelling, jokes, poems, ocarina, singing, autoharp, piano, guitar, harmonica, and so much more?

If all of this were not enough, on the Sunday afternoon we were moved by a special trip to the Bainbridge Island Japanese American Exclusion Memorial, the first location in the United States where Japanese Americans were forcefully removed to internment camps during World War II. We were fortunate to have a guided tour of the memorial park by Lily Kodama (filling in at the last minute when Clarence Moriwaki was unable to lead the tour), and then drove to nearby Winslow to visit the Bainbridge Island Historical Museum, where we viewed a documentary on the Manzanar WWII internment camp and saw the photography exhibit, "Ansel Adams: A Portrait of Manzanar." We then gathered at the new Bainbridge Island Art Museum for "Haiku Travels," a public reading by Terry Ann Carter, Marco Fraticelli, and Michael Dylan Welch, and an open-mic reading, complete with displays of handmade haiku books by Terry Ann plus sumi-e and haiga by Puget Sound Sumi Artists, coordinated by Dorothy Matthews. Such rich weekends our Seabeck haiku retreats are, as you can see. Here's a poem by Marco Fraticelli from this very full weekend:

> butterflies
> wasting my time
> writing haiku

2014

In 2014, we again held our Seabeck retreat near the height of autumn colors, October 16 to 19. This year marked the 100th anniversary of the Seabeck Conference Center, and we were treated to a special history presentation by Seabeck Conference Center executive director, Chuck Kraining. We again met at the Colman Center, and our theme song was "Getaway" by Earth, Wind and Fire ("So come, take me by the hand, we'll leave this troubled land. Get away!"). Registration remained at $215, and we had a record 57 attendees. This was the first year that Angela Terry joined Michael Dylan Welch in running the retreat, serving as our capable registrar, making sure that everyone was properly registered for all or part of the weekend, and assigned to their preferred overnight accommodations.

This year also began a new tradition that would last for five years, exploring each of the five senses in turn. We began in 2014 with the sense of sound, with many of our activities for the weekend emphasizing sound, such as Susan Constable's Thursday-night workshop, "Writing Sound Haiku," "Sounds and Other Senses," a nature walk led by Ruth Yarrow, and "400 Years of Sound in Japanese

Haiku" by Richard Tice. Aubrie Cox also led a workshop on "Musicality in Haibun Prose."

Our featured guest this year was Alan Pizzarelli, who began with a reading from his new best-of haiku and senryu collection, *Frozen Socks*. He continued with "American Haiku: A Personal Perspective from the Late Sixties to Today," a freeform reminiscence of poets who played major roles in developing and popularizing English-language haiku poetry—he seemed to know them all! This session was so bountiful it could have gone on for many more hours (who knew that Alan and *Haiku Handbook* author William J. Higginson used to be roommates?). Together with his partner, Donna Beaver, Alan also talked about their podcast, "Haiku Chronicles: A Continued Journey into Multimedia and Podcasting" (some of their recordings at the 2014 Seabeck retreat would be featured in later podcasts). Alan also gave a senryu presentation titled "Monkeys Invade the Sacred Palace and Chase Out the Tiger." He also participated in a panel discussion, "Haiku as Poetry," led by Aubrie Cox, which also included Deborah P Kolodji, John Stevenson, and Michael Dylan Welch, exploring the perception of haiku by the larger poetry community and how this perception has evolved.

Margaret D. McGee also made another labyrinth, and led meditations before breakfast each morning with labyrinth walks. Other activities included "A Haiku Trip to Japan" by Michael Dylan Welch, about his most recent visit (including a trip to Bashō's birthplace in Iga Ueno), and anonymous workshops by Kathy Munro and Deborah P Kolodji. Kathy, visiting from Whitehorse, also talked about the "Gift of the Land: Yukon Seasons." Susan Callan led us in a craft workshop, "Make a Flag Book: An Elegant Haiku Keeper," and master quilter RaNae Merrill talked about and displayed her elegant "Haikuilts," a combination of classic haiku and some of her own with detailed quilt designs.

We enjoyed haiku readings by Deborah P Kolodji, Tanya McDonald, John Stevenson, Aubrie Cox, Christopher Herold, and Karma Tenzing Wangchuk, plus a featured reading of haiku and senryu from Haiku Northwest's recently published 25th anniversary anthology, *No Longer Strangers*. Michelle Schaefer coordinated the reading, with music by James Rodriguez.

John Stevenson (our first featured guest to make a repeat visit) gave a workshop titled "Editor: Gatekeeper and Mentor," putting us in the position of being an editor for a haiku journal, considering a hypothetical submission. Carole MacRury introduced us to "Poems from the Shuswap: Haiku by Laryalee Fraser," with help from Susan Constable, and Terry Ann Carter facilitated a moving workshop, "Chiyo-ni and Aisatsu: Composing Greeting Haiku."

Our Friday-night highlight was perhaps one of the most magical events in our history. We were each given round paper lanterns with a blue tea light inside, and were invited to take a walk in the dark. In keeping with our weekend theme of sound, we did this walk in complete silence. What made the experience so magical was seeing dozens of haiku poets in a line, each carrying large round paper lanterns in the dark, all in silence, except for the persistent rain—and even the rain added to the event's aura, as if we were pilgrims determined to overcome any hardship or complication. We filed quietly across the wooden bridge to the antique store by the marina where he could hear

Hood Canal's splashing waves. We then silently crossed the wooden bridge again, and diverted to the boardwalk for a stop at what I like to call the moonviewing platform. We next walked in spirals through the labyrinth, and then headed up to the Cathedral in the Woods. There we finally began to talk, quietly, sharing some of our thoughts about the experience and reciting a few stray haiku—and Angela Terry rewarded us with chocolate truffles.

Other events during the weekend included a t'ai chi break and rengay writing, both of which we'd had before. Additional events included "Should the First Be Last," a haiku revision workshop led by Deborah P Kolodji, inviting us to consider the reversal of lines, and a "Haiku on Steroids" workshop directed by Michael Dylan Welch, where we made lists of haiku taboos or rules we typically wouldn't break and then wrote poems deliberately on those taboos or breaking those rules.

As usual, kukai voting, renkurama writing and reading, and Porad contest announcements brightened the weekend, and of course our shared meals in the dining hall are always an unsung gratification, as are the trifolds and other freebies on our freebie table, and copious snacks. Michael Dylan Welch had his "Haikuseum" on display, too, with boxes to open, poem cards to read, and other interactions.

Our Saturday night featured another rousing talent show, a surprise highlight of which was Barbara Hay introducing us to palm pipes. She gave each of us a plastic pipe, color-coded by length. We hit the end of the pipe on our palms, matching the pipe color to colors on a projected musical score. What fun music we made together, in such an unexpected way. After the talent show came "A Gala

Roast of Michael Dylan Welch," hosted by the one and only Joey Clifton (Alan Pizzarelli in disguise), with ignoble contributions by Donna Beaver and many other poets in attendance. A recording was made of this event but has mysteriously failed to surface.

On the Sunday, we heard from Jessica Tremblay, again our cartoonist-in-residence, with "Old Pond Comics: Out of the Woods," replete with fresh-off-the-laptop comics about our retreat. On the Sunday afternoon we again visited the Bainbridge Island Art Museum, enjoying a tour of current exhibitions, followed by a reception for Haiku Northwest in celebration of its new *No Longer Strangers* anthology. In addition to readings from that book, we also enjoyed haiku and senryu from Donna Beaver and Alan Pizzarelli (with Native American flute and harmonica), as well as poems from Aubrie Cox, Bob Moyer, John Stevenson, and Michael Dylan Welch, plus an open mic.

After the retreat, Chandra Bales and Susan Constable served as editors for *Rainsong*, our 2014 anthology, featuring haiga and sumi-e by Melinda Brottem, Darlene Dihel, Judy Kalin, Fumiko Kimura, Dorothy Matthews, and Nora Shannon—we remain grateful, as before, for their contributions to the Puget Sound Sumi Artists exhibit in the dining hall. The following is one of Alan Pizzarelli's poems from the weekend:

> in the still silence
> the slow fall
> of cottonwood seeds

2015

Our 2015 retreat took place earlier than usual, over the weekend of October 1 to 4, with fall colors just beginning, and featured Randy M. Brooks. We again met at the Colman Center, our registration fee was slightly higher at $225, and we collected 50 attendees. Our theme song this year was a soaring jazz guitar instrumental, "Praise," by Pat Metheny. The attitude of praise lies behind many haiku, and it seemed a suitable way to celebrate our common poetic passion.

Our theme for the weekend was the sense of touch, which manifested itself immediately on the opening night in "Getting in Touch: Breaking the Ice" facilitated by Katharine Grubb, followed by the "Haiku Handshake," where we lined up to shake hands with everyone else in attendance. Lots of hugs, too. Michael Dylan Welch led us in a group discussion on "The Meanings of Touch," and facilitated a workshop on "The Finishing Touch: Cutting Haiku" while Tanya McDonald gave a beginner workshop. Other touch-related presentations included "Feeling the Flow: A Touch of T'ai Chi" demonstrated by Elizabeth-Ann Winkler, "Keeping in Touch with International Haiku Poets" by Carmen Sterba, and "Touching and Touched: The Body's Experience," facilitated by Erica Akiko Howard, a gentle movement exercise designed to bring awareness to the body as the instrument of touch—immediately followed by a backrub break for those who wanted to participate. Kathabela Wilson facilitated "Touch Notes," Richard Tice led us through "Four Hundred Years of Touchy-Feely Japanese Haiku," and Angela Terry gave a presentation on "Touching Japan." Jacquie Pearce also got us going with "Erotic Haiku: A Hands-On Workshop."

Perhaps the most tactile of our touching weekend activities, though, was "Bagging It: Hands-In Writing Workshop." Angela Terry and Michael Dylan Welch gave each participant a paper bag and asked them to feel inside the bag, without looking, and to write haiku in response to what they felt—buttons, walnuts, thimbles, coins, and who knows what else. Initial apprehension quickly turned to engaged chattering and the inspiration for many poems.

We also heard haiku readings by Michelle Schaefer and Ce Rosenow, and the "One Breath Poets" group from Bend, Oregon (Janet Whitney, Sandy Thompson, and Lorna Cahall), at the Cathedral in the Woods. Ce also gave a talk on "Caring Imagination: Haikai and Care Ethics," and Patty Hardin introduced us to "Taking the Buson Challenge." Other presentations included an "Ink, Brush, Paper" haiga presentation by Annette Makino, and an overview of "Haiga on Tanzaku Scrolls" by Dorothy Matthews. As usual, we also had renkurama and rengay writing, an anonymous workshop, our kukai, the Porad contest winners announcement, a group photo, and talent show, plus a "Slow Ginko" (haiku walk) led by Michael. Completely unusual was that we spotted a Pacific spiny dogfish (a type of bottom-feeding shark) in the lagoon!

Randy M. Brooks gave us our chief weekend highlights, though, starting with his Thursday-night haiku reading. He also talked about "A Life Touched by Haiku: Forty Years of Writing, Editing, Publishing, and Teaching," detailing a remarkable career of tremendous influence in English-language haiku poetry. His featured presentation was

"American Haiku: A Century Filled with Experimentation," followed by a break-the-mold workshop in writing experimental haiku. He left us with "The Haiku Blessing," about the intimate ways haiku invite us to be touched by other's lives, perceptions, sensations, and shared insights.

For 2015, our anthology editors were Dianne Garcia, Tanya McDonald, and Angela Terry, and the numbered, handbound collection they produced was titled *Exhaling*. Here's a poem from the book by Randy M. Brooks:

> fog settles over the bay
> the retreat center
> breakfast bell

2016

The sense of smell guided our next Seabeck Haiku Getaway, this being our next theme taken from the five primary senses. The 2016 retreat took place from October 27 to 30, once again at the Colman Center—our last time there. The theme song went a bit campy this year, with "Stop and Smell the Roses" by Ringo Starr ("Why don't I just stop, look at the pretty roses, smell them for one moment, take the time to see?"). This year's retreat attracted 59 attendees, a new record number, but the fee to register remained at $225.

Our featured guest was scholar and translator Sonja Arntzen. She read some of her own haiku on the opening evening, and gave thought-provoking presentations on "Sniffing Out Haiku in the Waka Tradition," "Associative Linking: An Aesthetic Constant in Japanese Literature," and "Uta-makura: Place as a Pillow for Poetry." The first talk gave us a larger and older context for our haiku habit. The second talk prepped us for our collaborative writing to come, and the third talk inspired us to make stronger use of place names in our haiku as a means of giving our work richer meaning and greater compression. As already suggested, Sonja also inspired us in a renku-writing session, titled "Four Sheets to the Seabeck Wind." Her instructions said, "The rules are to make it a game and therefore fun. Give the rules your best shot, but if it stops being fun, start breaking the rules." Joining Sonja for the weekend was her husband, Richard John Lynn, a scholar and translator of Chinese literature, who talked about "Image and Imagination in the Chinese Poetic Tradition."

This year we began mini-writing exercises called "Write Now," each with a minute or so to explain a prompt, ten minutes of writing, and a few more minutes to share what we came up with. We had had "Write Now" sessions in 2015, but they were longer exercises. This year's "Write Now" activities were just fifteen minutes each (in subsequent years they would be shortened to ten minutes), and were provided by Angela Terry ("The Scent of Song"), Michael Dylan Welch ("The Stink of Politics," focusing on senryu), Chandra Bales ("The Scent of the Season"), Lynne Jambor ("The Scent of Cooking"), John Stevenson ("The Scent of Childhood"), Johnny Baranski ("Goblins and Ghosts," in celebration of our Halloween weekend), Carolyn Winkler and Angela Terry ("The Scent of the Dead," in acknowledgment of the Day of the Dead), and Vicki McCullough ("The Scent of Memory"). These sessions enabled us to do more haiku writing than in some of our previous retreats, and mostly emphasized the weekend theme.

Also connecting to the theme was "Making Sense of Smell," a writing workshop led by Angela and Michael, using small containers of smelly things (mostly nice—but with a few olfactory surprises) to inspire fresh writing. We also enjoyed "The Scent of Japanese Haiku," a presentation of haiku translations by Richard Tice. Over the years Richard has gifted us with many fine explorations of Japanese haiku, all with his own translations, and we are particularly grateful for his knowledge and research in this area.

Fittingly for this spooky time of the year, Jacquie Pearce led a haiku workshop on "Halloween and Horror," followed by a "Zombie shoulder-rub break" (you'll have to imagine that). We also had a "Mask-Making" Halloween craft activity led by Angela and Carolyn, followed up during our talent show with a mask dance and procession. Katharine Grubb MC'd our talent show in fine style, orchestrating elaborate Halloween decorations and dressing up in costume, with much help from others.

Before all this, Darlene Dihel and Dorothy Matthews gave a short talk on "Haiga and Sumi-e," in support of this year's haiga exhibit by the Haiga Adventure Study Group of Puget Sound Sumi Artists. Other presentations included a "Scent and Memory" haibun workshop by Margaret Chula, at the same time as Michael's "Haiku Targets" workshop for beginners. We were also privileged to hear "My Australian Haiku" by Leanne Mumford, who was visiting us from Down Under. A special treat was "Photographing Haiku," presented by Hisao Mogi, president of the Rainier Haiku

Ginsha, Seattle's Japanese-language haiku group (Hisao is also an accomplished photographer).

Jay Friedenberg gave us "Painting Haiku," a reading and art presentation. Other featured readings were shared by Dianne Garcia, Margaret Chula, and Leanne Mumford. And, in the Cathedral in the Woods, we also heard haiku and senryu by the Portland Haiku Group (Shelley Baker-Gard, Johnny Baranski, James Rodriguez, and Carolyn Winkler), plus readings by Chandra Bales, Barbara Snow, Chrissi Villa (from her new book *The Bluebird's Cry*), and Michael Dylan Welch and Tanya McDonald (from their new book *Seven Suns / Seven Moons*).

Terran Campbell, Tanya, and Angela also led a moving memorial reading for longtime Haiku Northwest member Marilyn Sandall. Angela Naccarato inspired us with an innovative craft activity, "Haiku Rocks," in which we penned or painted haiku on specially selected and prepared stones. David Berger gave an informative and timely presentation "All About Mushrooms," and then led us on a nature walk to hunt for specimens. The mushrooms seemed especially cooperative this year, too. Michael Dylan Welch talked about "The Weather-Beaten Jizo: Shikoku Pilgrimage Haiku by Shuji Niwano," complete with maps, photographs, and a bush warbler sound recording to go with pilgrimage haiku. Speaking of Japan, Annette Makino and her daughter Maya shared "Journey to Japan: A Haiku Travelogue," documenting their recent family trip to the home of haiku. And to make sure we stayed in a Japanese mood, Ellen Ankenbrock, Shelley Baker-Gard, and Carolyn Winkler gave us "First You Boil Water," a full-blown tea ceremony, with tea and sweets for all. And lest they be forgotten, we held a pair of anonymous workshops, more late-night rengay writing, announced the 2016 Porad contest winners, sold books and other items in our book fair and silent auction, exercised our haiku judgment in the annual kukai, and posed together for the group photo.

The outstanding highlight of the weekend, undoubtedly one of the most memorable activities in our retreat history, was a Saturday night walk to the cemetery. We sauntered through the woods for fifteen minutes, occasionally stepping around large puddles in the trail, and then explored the dark and sometimes overgrown gravestones with flashlights. After half an hour, those who came gathered in a large semicircle outside the cemetery's wooden fence. There we stood silently for a few minutes, invited to contemplate our mortality. After a few quiet minutes, a distant singing bowl began to ring, and then came a mournful flute. As we stood in silence a white-robed ghost of a figure emerged from the woods, while the flute music played, and the figure quietly handed out large printout posters of *jisei*, or death haiku, one to each person present. Not a word was spoken as we read each poem by flashlight, such as this by Koyo, who died in 1903: "if I must die / let it be autumn / when the dew is dry," or this by Ensetsu, who died in 1743: "autumn gust— / I have no further business / in this world." Then as soon as the ethereal magic started, it drew to a close, as the robed figure (Michelle Schaefer) disappeared into the dark in the direction of the music (played by James Rodriguez). We had all been transformed as we found our way back to the meeting room for the evening's talent show, themed on Halloween and the Day of the Dead—although with many departures, such as another ukulele chorus.

Our 2016 anthology editors, Ce Rosenow and Barbara Snow, featured poems capturing these and many other moments in *Inhaling*, titled as a response to the 2015 anthology, *Exhaling*. Here's a poem from the 2016 book, by Sonja Arntzen, whose quiet, gentle authority warmed us all weekend:

by the lagoon
wild pears—no fragrance . . .
bitter taste too

2017

And so we come to our tenth anniversary retreat, our first to be held in the Meeting House, a larger facility that gave us much more room for our attendees (52 this year) and all our displays and activities. Our 2017 getaway took place October 26 to 29, with taste as our theme. Our theme song was Ravel's "Boléro," a fitting musical metaphor for how everyone comes together for each Seabeck weekend, each one of us adding a distinctive voice to our mounting crescendo in celebration of haiku. Michael Dylan Welch and Angela Terry continued as retreat director and registrar, and our registration fee rose to $240. Though the fees were higher this year, we'd strived each year to make them as lean as possible. The fee was $199 in 2010, the first year the retreat stretched to three nights, so an increase of only $41 over that time has not been great, and we're grateful to the Seabeck Conference Center for providing such inspiring and versatile facilities at such a reasonable cost.

After our usual opening-night welcome and round of introductions, Scott Mason, our featured guest, launched us into a reading of his haiku, with "A Taste of Sound Play." His other talks included "Haiku: A State of Wonder" and a haiku workshop, "Tap into Wonder," both in support of his new book, *The Wonder Code*, at once an anthology of haiku and a how-to book for writing out of a sense of amazement. As his book emphasizes in its epigraph from Abraham Joshua Heschel, "The beginning of our happiness lies in the understanding that life without wonder is not worth living." Scott also led us in an overview of "Dandelion Globes and Hand Grenades—Haiku that Move Us" and contributed to a panel discussion on "Personal Taste in Haiku," which also featured Terry Ann Carter, John Stevenson, and Michael.

Richard Tice expounded on our weekend theme with "A Taste of Japanese Haiku," with more of his translations, and Angela led us on an experiential writing workshop, titled "A Taste of Haiku," in which samples of items to taste got us writing. James Rodriguez also led us in "Taste the Wind: Haiku Kites," an engaging craft workshop where we put together handmade kites, each one decorated with haiku. Some of us ventured outdoors to give our haiku kites test flights, while others were able to make short runs indoors to get their kites aloft.

We had four anonymous workshops this year, led by Michael, Susan Constable, Lynne Jambor, and Johnny Baranski. Nicholas Klacsanzky led early risers in morning meditations, before breakfast, and we enjoyed a new slate of "Write Now" exercises, this time led by Michelle Schaefer ("Unsavory Characters"), Elehna de Sousa ("Food for the Soul"), Kathabela Wilson ("Family Stew," with flute music by Rick Wilson), Ruth Marcus ("Ekphrastic Mandala Haiku," with displays of her stunning mandala artwork), and Michael ("Seasonal Food Words"). Most of these exercises catered to the taste theme. As you can see elsewhere in this book's pages, this theme produced many tasty haiku.

Still more presentations included "On the Tokaido Road" by Terry Ann, "Savoring/Savouring Anna Vakar: Book Launch and Remembrance" by Vicki McCullough, "Introducing Haiku" by Tanya McDonald, at the same time as Michael's "Haiku Is _____" discussion (in which he didn't say a single word), "Buried Treasure: Hood Canal and Haiku" by David Berger (from his University of Washington Press book about razor clams), "Mathematical Thoughts in Ancient Chinese Poems" by Hao Shen, visiting from China (a unexpected delight), and "Skywriting: Learning Haiku from Annie Dillard" by Michael.

Readings for the weekend, again at the Cathedral in the Woods, began with poems by contributors to Scott Mason's *The Wonder Code* (Johnny Baranski, Susan Constable, Ida Freilinger, Tanya, Barbara Snow, John Stevenson, Angela, Michael, and Kathabela Wilson), introduced by Scott. We also heard from Elehna de Sousa ("Gossamer Threads") and Nicholas Klacsanzky (from his book *Zen and Son*, much of which also featured work by his father, George Klacsanzky, whose pioneering haiku activities in the Seattle area laid some of the groundwork for Francine Porad's formation of Haiku Northwest in 1988). Later, Julie Emerson, David Berger, and Jacquie Pearce read us "Ripe," a kasen renku they'd been working on since the previous year's retreat.

A highlight of the weekend was an "Etegami Postcard Painting Workshop," led by Darlene Dihel, assisted by Dorothy Matthews and Melinda Brottem, in which we each created artwork in the etegami tradition, a sort of casual haiga where rapid paintings are paired with inspiring words (not necessarily haiku). We enjoyed seeing everyone's creations, especially those by Darlene, Dorothy, and Melinda, throughout the weekend.

We also enjoyed two nature walks, one to the waterfront, and another we called "Seabeck Discoveries," where everyone was invited to discover the friendship garden, the totem pole, the bouncy bridge, the sundial, and other hidden gems around the campus. As usual, we enjoyed rengay writing, announcing the 2017 Porad Award winners, another group photo and kukai, and a talent show—where it is so easy to read those two words, but nearly impossible to grasp the range, quality, and joy of the talent shared. One tradition that's been part of our talent shows, for example, is what we have called a "sing-off." In this friendly competition, haiku and senryu by our featured guest are put into a hat to be drawn at random by willing victims who take turns coming up with a spontaneous way to sing each poem—heavy metal, country, opera, any style goes. We've had fun dividing the audience into two halves to compete for the loudest laughs and mightiest applause.

Meanwhile, back for the third time as our Seabeck cartoonist in residence, Jessica Tremblay presented "Seabeck Comics," including freshly produced comics all about our weekend. If you search for her Seabeck haiku comics online, you'll see how she's captured the spirit and details of our retreats, now having reached a full ten years. We look forward to all the new territory we'll explore in the next ten years, perhaps going even farther than we can imagine, as in this poem by Scott Mason:

> full moon
> one giant leap
> for a water strider

And now, in your hands, you hold the 2017 Seabeck Haiku Getaway anthology, *Seabeck Reunion*, edited by Michael Dylan Welch. We hope you might join our next Seabeck reunion, for it always feels like coming home, even if you've never attended before.

Reunion Participants

Ellen Ankenbrock / Portland, Oregon 54, 73

Sonja Arntzen / Gabriola Island, British Columbia. 27, 124

Shelley Baker-Gard / Portland, Oregon 52, 64, 84

Johnny Baranski / Vancouver, Washington 5, 55, 71, 77, 92

David Berger / Seattle, Washington 46, 51, 53, 80, 87, 95

Nancy Bright / Sisters, Oregon 42, 72

Randy M. Brooks / Taylorville, Illinois 26, 119

Susan M. Callan / Bainbridge Island, Washington 61, 65

Terran Campbell / Seattle, Washington 51, 62

Terry Ann Carter / Victoria, British Columbia. 44, 53, 93

Lysa Collins / White Rock, British Columbia. 53, 74, 75

Susan Constable / Parksville, British Columbia. 67, 83, 84, 95

Eileen Coughlin / Bellingham, Washington. 49, 76

Marion Davidson / Bend, Oregon 56, 82

elehna de sousa / Salt Spring Island, British Columbia. 38, 43, 61

Darlene Dihel / Enumclaw, Washington .80

Julie Emerson / Vancouver, British Columbia 33, 40

Gary Evans / Stanwood, Washington 61, 63, 79

Marco Fraticelli / Valois, Québec. 25, 112

Ida Freilinger / Redmond, Washington 34, 41

Dianne Garcia / Seattle, Washington 33, 49, 57, 91

Penny Harter / Mays Landing, New Jersey. 23, 101

Barbara Ellen Hay / Tulsa, Oklahoma. 35, 39, 55, 94

Connie Hutchison / Kirkland, Washington 39, 45, 83

Lynne Jambor / Vancouver, British Columbia 34, 36, 38

Susan M. Kerr / Bainbridge Island, Washington 31, 37, 67

Nicholas Klacsanzky / Edmonds, Washington 72, 75, 78

Ruth La Sure / Chicago, Illinois. 73, 85

Ruth Marcus / Sequim, Washington. 72, 81

Scott Mason / Chappaqua, New York 27, 45, 65, 66, 93, 128

Dorothy Avery Matthews / Poulsbo, Washington 32, 50, 65

Vicki McCullough / Vancouver, British Columbia 68, 83, 87, 92

Tanya McDonald / Woodinville, Washington 44, 71, 82

Paul Miller / Bristol, Rhode Island 25, 108

Emiko Miyashita / Kawasaki, Japan 23, 99

Jacquie Pearce / Vancouver, British Columbia 31, 34, 67, 87, 91

Alan Pizzarelli / Bloomfield, New Jersey 26, 116

Laura Quindt / Woodinville, Washington 76, 78, 85

Rayn Roberts / Lynnwood, Washington. 66, 80

Jim Rodriguez / Washougal, Washington 36, 42, 87

Jacob Salzer / Vancouver, Washington 37, 77, 86, 93

Michelle Schaefer / Bothell, Washington. 44, 63, 84, 87

Barbara Snow / Eugene, Oregon 40, 77, 81

John Stevenson / Nassau, New York 9–11, 24, 50, 51, 104

Angela Terry / Lake Forest Park, Washington 54, 57, 75

Kathleen Tice / Kent, Washington 73, 79

Richard Tice / Kent, Washington 32, 56, 66, 95

Kay L. Tracy / Portland, Oregon 35, 55, 74

Jessica Tremblay / Burnaby, British Columbia 35, 40, 43

Charles Trumbull / Santa Fe, New Mexico 24, 103

Michael Dylan Welch / Sammamish, Washington . . . .
. . . . .13–20, 32, 43, 64, 87, 94, 97–128

Janet Whitney / Bend, Oregon 74, 82, 86

Kath Abela Wilson / Pasadena, California 38, 43, 52

Rick Wilson / Pasadena, California. .41, 81

www.ingramcontent.com/pod-product-compliance
Lightning Source LLC
Chambersburg PA
CBHW080518090426
42734CB00015B/3097